A Wom

Intermittent Fasting

How I Dropped 30 Pounds And How You Can Do It Too!

By

Evelyn Whitbeck

Table Of Contents

Introduction

Dieting is hard. Especially in the current climate where new information appears second-by-second, dieting feels like a never-ending cycle of trying to figure out what works and what does not work because the recommendations so drastically change. One day researchers say drinking coffee is going to help me live longer; the next day, they say coffee is poison and should be avoided at all costs. Okay, maybe the conflicting information is not *that* dramatic. But, choosing the right diet plan is painstaking when you are a woman trying to lose weight and are drowning in articles without a clue about which plan to choose.

I was that drowning woman while I was sitting in my office one morning and a colleague of mine casually mentioned he was fasting for the day. Charles, as I will call him, is the type who normally has a goodie in one hand and a cup of coffee in the other, so the thought of him fasting caught me off guard. My eyes squinted with curiosity as I looked him up and down and asked, "Why on earth are you fasting?" He informed me he enjoys fasting for 24 hours once per week to "reset his system" which I took to mean energy, metabolism, and overall well-being. I thought to myself, *now that is an interesting form of torture.* But the interaction intrigued me enough to learn more.

Having studied nutrition for years and working in a previous life as a menu creator for a meal delivery service, I did not believe fasting was healthy. What I did not realize is there are countless ways to practice fasting that does not involve self-inflicted starvation. What my friend Charles was practicing is called *Intermittent Fasting,* and it is a form of fasting but completely different at the same time.

With intermittent fasting, the fasting periods are short and spread throughout the week. Also, the health benefits linked to intermittent fasting would persuade even the most disbelieving of disbelievers to try it. I tried it. Moreover, I genuinely love the results. I did not have to drastically change my diet, I have so much more energy, my work has improved because I think with greater clarity, and I finally lost the weight I have been trying to get off for years.

Now it is your turn to look and feel better through the secret I discovered during a coincidental office conversation. This book is going to show women who have tried everything to lose weight and have all but given up how fasting can be easily incorporated into any lifestyle to help shed those stubborn pounds off. I was in your shoes not long ago, and now that I know how strong and healthy my body can feel by making a simple lifestyle change, I wish I had started long ago. Do not waste another second debating what diet fad to try next; read on and join this journey with me.

Intermittent Fasting

What Is Intermittent Fasting?

In case you are unfamiliar with the term, fasting simply means to refrain from consuming food and specific beverages for an extended period of time. People have practiced fasting for centuries; historically, it was used to achieve spiritual healing or to reap health benefits like weight loss and insulin regulation [1]. Depending on the culture, religion, geographic region, and other individual characteristics, fasting takes different forms. For example, certain religions practice fasting from food, beverage, or both, for certain periods of time for the purpose of hyperfocused prayer and becoming closer to the chosen God or deity [2]. Non-religious fasting is even more varied as it not only comes in different forms but often serves different purposes as well.

Intermittent fasting (IF) is a specific form of fasting during which an individual does not consume calories for a period of hours or days, but then resumes their normal diet during the remaining hours or days [3]. Often what attracts people to IF is that it doesn't necessarily restrict *what* to eat, rather it dictates *when* to eat by incorporating short-term fasting periods into a normal day [4]. The only exception to this is when weight loss is the motivation for practicing IF, in which case I am sorry to be the bearer of bad news, but IF is not magically going to help you lose weight without minding what you eat.

Even though IF inherently cuts down on the number of meals being eaten, it is still recommended that you maintain healthy eating habits if your goal in practicing IF is weight loss [3]. Because this may very well be the goal for most of you seeing as to how you picked up this book: don't fret! What I am *not* saying is that you will have to eat broccoli and cabbage every day to lose weight while practicing IF. What I *am* saying, however, is that IF is a holistic lifestyle change that incorporates short-term periods of fasting into eating healthy most of the time while still indulging a little bit of the time and seeing results. In addition, remember, we are in this together. We will discuss weight loss hacks while practicing IF and provide a 10-day sample 16/8 Method of IF that will help catapult your weight loss goals in a later chapter.

Women And Intermittent Fasting

Unique Considerations

As a modern-day informed woman, before embarking on IF I immediately started looking for articles, books, blogs, and any information I could find to get started. Although I found many resources on IF in general, I was disappointed to realize there were minimal resources on IF specifically geared toward women. While I am all about gender equality and women being capable of doing everything men can do, I still understand my body is inherently different from a man's body. My caloric needs are different, my hormones are different (hello, menstruation!), and my metabolism is different meaning I may need a different IF setup than a man. Naturally, I decided to write this book for other women seeking similar, specific information on how to practice IF as a woman in a healthy way.

Despite a plethora of evidence on the positive effects of IF that we went over in the previous chapter, the practice of fasting effects women differently than men [5] [6]. So far, with what limited research exists on human subjects and IF, the outcomes for men have all been quite positive while the outcomes for women have been mixed [5]. For example, one study found that IF led to worse blood sugar control in women compared to men after a 22-day, alternate-day fast [6]. The same study also showed improvement in insulin insensitivity in men, while women did not experience the same improvement [6]. However, in another study IF was shown to encourage weight loss and reduce the risk of coronary heart disease among obese women [7].

Other information regarding women and IF is not in the form of human subject research studies, rather in studies performed on female rodents. Results in these rodent studies have suggested that practicing IF as a woman may lead to emaciation [8], irregular or missed menstrual cycles [9] loss of bone density and reduction of ovary size in addition to other negative health effects [9]. Before you get worried and start to wonder why you would consider starting an IF plan, remember that these results were seen in rodents, not humans. And, also remember that you can modify your IF plan to avoid these concerns by creating a plan that works specifically for your body. Put a pin in these topics because we will go more into depth on them in a minute.

With the tremendous popularity of personal blogs, Youtube channels, and social media outlets, there are more anecdotal accounts of women telling their personal experiences of practicing IF than you could get through in a lifetime. Although it is not particularly scientific, this anecdotal information on the ins and outs, pros and cons, results, and other details about specific IF types that women have tried is critical because there is such a lack of scientific study on the subject. With this being said, be wary of information provided by people or products who want you to buy something. Those who are out for profit wanting you to buy their book, supplements, or pay for some kind of information they have may tell you anything you want to hear to pocket your money. If the results seem too good to be true, they probably are.

Despite the potential health concerns that women may experience while practicing IF, women without medical or health concerns can and are encouraged to participate in IF. The take-home message is that women need to be informed, in-tune with their bodies, and practice modified forms of IF with fewer and/or shorter fasting periods to avoid potential harm [4]. The only exceptions to this "women can do" attitude includes women who are pregnant, breastfeeding, or trying to conceive. Please wait until you have surpassed these (wonderful) health events to attempt any sort of fasting regimen to preserve enough nutrients to support your own health and the health of the child dependent on you for their nutrition [4]. Additionally, women who are underweight or malnourished, or have a history of eating disorders, diabetes or low blood sugar, or amenorrhea (irregular periods) should refrain from IF [4].

Fasting And Hormones

Women's bodies are sensitive to calorie deprivation, and in evolutionary terms, this is for good reason [10]. When a woman's body senses starvation, whether intentional or not, the body will automatically increase production of the hunger hormones called leptin and ghrelin [11]. The purpose of this enhanced hormone response is to send a signal to the woman to eat because, well, she is starving, and her body wants her to fix it. Another more evolutionary reason for this hormone response is the body's way of ensuring the woman eats to protect her potential fetus [10]. The most amazing part about this is it happens even when a woman is not pregnant! This is how protective women's bodies are of their fertility and creating an internal environment amenable to nurturing offspring in the womb.

In addition to the enhanced production of hunger hormones, fasting for too long or too frequently can impact a part of the brain called the hypothalamus, leading to a cascade of other hormonal events [12]. These events have to do with hormone secretion or more specifically, disrupting the secretion of the gonadotropin-releasing hormone or GnRH. This matters for women because GnRH is responsible for releasing two reproductive hormones called the luteinizing hormone or LH and the follicle stimulating hormone or FSH [10]. When this process of releasing essential hormones is disrupted, it can lead to a host of negative health outcomes for women including irregular menstrual cycles, loss of bone density, infertility, and mental health concerns including depression and anxiety [10] [13].

Additional research on the effect IF can have on women's hormones includes a study on female rodents subjected to 3-6 months of alternate-day fasting [8]. The results of this study showed after 6 months, female rats became emaciated, displayed heightened stress response, and reproductive shut down in the form of reduced ovary size and irregular menstrual cycles [8]. Interestingly, this study also found improvement in female rodent learning and memory after 6 months of alternate-day fasting, attributed to the evolutionary ability of women to survive during periods of nutrient scarcity [8]. While the cognitive results were positive, the breadth of the negative results is indicative of why choosing modified versions of IF is imperative for women.

Metabolic Disturbance

Fasting and metabolism have a complicated relationship. On one hand, fasting for too long that leads to starvation can wreak havoc on metabolism because it sends the body into a state of nutrient preservation. In this state, the body holds onto fat as energy to survive, and metabolism drops to further protect energy for survival [14]. However, modified fasting like IF that lasts for shorter periods of time can actually improve metabolism and metabolic disorders [15]. One study performed on 11 healthy men found an increase in their resting metabolism by 14% after an 84-hour fast under otherwise normal living conditions [16]. But, the same research has not been performed on women.

This fine line between metabolic detriment and benefit due to fasting, along with limited metabolic IF research geared toward women, are more reasons why it is so important that women choose a type of IF that works for their individual needs. There is no one modified fasting method (IF) that has been identified as "optimal" for metabolism in terms of how much caloric restriction is necessary during fasting, how many days are spent fasting, how long fasting is sustained, and eating habits on nonfasting days [15]. And even if there was one designated type of IF that was found to be the most beneficial for metabolic health, it is likely this type would not produce the same results for every woman. This is because metabolism, just like hormones, is different for every woman. In fact, metabolism and hormones are interconnected, which is why they are both concerns for women while practicing IF [17]. Let's shift gears a bit and talk more about this relationship now.

The metabolic disturbance is an oft-cited concern for women practicing IF because of the hormonal shifts that may occur while fasting that we have already discussed. Remember the GnRH, FSH, and LH hormones? Well, they're back. During the menstrual cycle, the ovaries release an egg, and this is called ovulation [18]. Ovulation is far from all that is occurring during this time; simultaneously, the body is going through a plethora of other hormonal changes to prepare for the potential of becoming pregnant. For example, during this time the GnRH hormone is sent to the pituitary gland which triggers the pituitary gland to release the LH and FSH hormones to the ovaries to signal production of estrogen and progesterone [10]. I know this is a lot of information and some of it is repeated from the hormone segment (I told you metabolism and hormones are interconnected!) but stick with me we are getting to the point.

Recall how we said energy deficiency disrupts this hormone signaling process by the pituitary gland. Well, when this signaling process is disrupted, this means estrogen production is disrupted because estrogen production is reliant on the successful release of LH and FSH hormones [17]. Estrogen should actually be called estrogens (plural) because there are a few different metabolites of estrogen that circulate the body at different ratios throughout a woman's lifespan [19]. The 3 estrogen metabolites are: estriol, estradiol, and estrone [17] [19]. And, these 3 estrogens are not only imperative in the reproductive process, but are also responsible for regulating metabolism [19].

In premenopausal women, the estrogen metabolite called estradiol circulates the body at the highest proportion compared to estriol and estrone [19]. After menopause, the ratio of estradiol and the general ratio of circulating estrogens in the woman's body substantially decreases and this decrease is linked to increased fat storage and also to increased food consumption [17]. In common language, this refers to a woman's tendency to gain weight after menopause because her body is holding onto more fat and she may be consuming more calories, due to the level of circulating estrogens dropping. If you think about it, then, if fasting disrupts the process of estrogen production leading to a lower presence of estrogens circulating in a woman's body, it makes sense that this may lead to metabolic disturbance.

So, what is a metabolic disturbance anyway? It might sound scary, but when you pull apart the words, the phrase is quite straightforward. Metabolic or metabolism refers to the way our bodies convert food to energy [20]. Disturbance is another word for disruption of a process [20]. Putting these definitions together, metabolic disturbance simply refers to the disruption of the body's normal metabolic process [20]. In the case of estrogens, when lower than normal estrogens are circulating throughout a woman's body, this disrupts her normal metabolic functions because her body is burning less energy (i.e. holding onto more fat) at the same time she is consuming more energy due to the hormonal change. While this occurs naturally during menopause, this process can be kickstarted when the body is going through periods of energy deprivation like fasting [19].

Summary

In this chapter, we talked about IF as it specifically concerns women. Hopefully, by now you understand that IF effects men differently than women, and these differences are scientifically supported. There are risks associated with IF including hormonal and metabolic dysregulation, but there are benefits associated with IF including improved cognitive function and weight loss. The most important concept I hope you walk away from this chapter with is that while IF can be detrimental to women if practiced the wrong way, it can be extremely beneficial if you practice IF the right way according to your individual needs. IF is not just fasting and it is not self-induced starvation; in fact, these practices can lead to the detrimental health effects we talked about. IF is *modified* fasting that you can structure to fit your individual body's needs and lose weight and feel your best in a healthy way.

Types Of Intermittent Fasting

As previously mentioned, there are a variety of ways an individual may practice IF in terms of which forms of caloric intake are restricted and for how long [13]. For example, some types of IF call for complete restriction of solid food intake but allow water, black coffee, and other zero-calorie beverages during the fasting period. Other types of IF involve calorie restriction rather than complete fasting, such that food and beverage are allowed up to 500 and 600 calories on fasting days for men and women respectively [13]. The type of IF chosen is completely up to the individual and should ideally fit well with the individual's established schedule, workout regimen, metabolism, and any special dietary or medical requirements.

While the benefits of IF are scientifically-supported, which will be discussed shortly, practicing IF effects women differently than men [4]. In some studies, IF was not as effective in women as it was for men; in fact, one study showed poorer blood sugar regulation in women versus men who were practicing IF [6]. Another concern is the effect of IF on hormone dysregulation which may lead to a host of negative health outcomes including missed periods and loss of bone density, all discussed in a later chapter of this book [9]. Despite these unique health concerns, women can still practice IF; however, it is suggested that women ease into IF and practice modified IF types that incorporate fewer days of fasting and shorter fasting periods. These IF types include: Crescendo Method, 16/8, and Eat Stop Eat [4] [13].

The Crescendo Method of IF involves fasting for 12-16 hours over a period of 2-3 nonconsecutive days per week [4]. For instance, a woman may fast Monday, Wednesday, and Thursday for 12-16 hours perhaps between 8 pm the evening before until lunchtime the following day. She would then resume her normal dietary pattern the remainder of the day, and all day on Tuesday, Thursday, Saturday, and Sunday. To start with, a woman would be recommended to fast for 12 hours the first few days with this method, incrementally working up to the full 16-hour fast over time.

The 16/8 Method, also known as the "Leangains Method", involves fasting for 16 hours per day followed by consuming the days' worth of calories during the remaining 8 hours of the day [4]. On this Method, people typically prefer to stop eating after dinner between 7-8 pm and fast until the following day at lunchtime between 11am-12 pm. For women, it is recommended to begin this Method by fasting for 12-14 hours per day, incrementally working up to the full 16 hours of fasting per day.

The Eat Stop Eat Method, also known as the "24-hour protocol", is different than the previous two methods in that it entails a full 24-hour fast from all solid foods for 1-2 days per week [4]. During the fast, zero-calorie beverages like water, black coffee, and unsweetened tea are allowed. For women, the Stop Eat Stop Method is only recommended up to 2 days per week and fasting for 14-16 hours at a time in the beginning, incrementally working up to the full 24 hours overtime.

The Science Of Intermittent Fasting

Scientific literature is abundant with studies performed on rodents and humans showing associations between the practice of IF and specific health benefits like the prevention of aging and disease [13]. But oddly enough, scientists have not been able to identify the exact reason why IF produces these health benefits [21]. There are, of course, several theories behind IF's effectiveness being explored, though, and it seems scientists have pinpointed mainly the body's reaction to fasting as the most plausible explanation [21]. This is to say, when our body enters a state of nutrient deprivation, i.e. what happens during fasting, beneficial changes start happening in our cells. Three of the most commonly studied ways that these beneficial changes occur are: the activation of autophagy and ketogenesis, and the inherent reduction of caloric intake while practicing IF [21] [22].

Autophagy may sound complicated, but all it refers to is a process our cells undergo to keep internal balance [23]. Think of removing clutter and repairing broken items in your home every so often to maintain the quality of your living quarters; this is exactly what cells do to survive. During autophagy, cells self-degrade by removing dysfunctional or damaged organelles, proteins, and other intracellular pathogens to maintain its health [23] [24]. In addition to removing these dysfunctional intracellular materials, the cell can also recycle the discarded material to generate energy or for cellular renewal [23].

The autophagic process (i.e., autophagy) may be induced or accelerated during times of nutrient deprivation like starvation, fasting, exercising, or while the body is in a state of ketosis [25] [26]. When autophagy is induced under these circumstances (think: IF), the cellular response is to tap into intracellular nutrient reserves to generate internal energy for survival. The autophagic process has been linked to disease prevention including cancers, diabetes, autoimmune disorders, and Parkinson's, which is consequently why scientists think IF's ability to induce autophagy is so beneficial [27] [28].

Another cellular process that IF has been linked to is called ketosis [14]. This word may seem similarly daunting as autophagy at first, but it is simply the body's process of using an alternative form of energy while fasting [33]. An alternative form of energy is necessary because glucose (sugar) is depleted during periods of fasting, and as chances would have it, the body's preferred source of energy is glucose. Hence, the body must find some other source of energy to survive. Luckily due to evolution and the body's fascinating ability to adapt, the liver naturally produces ketones as an alternative source of energy during fasting, which accumulate in plasma [34] [35]. The production of ketones is called ketogenesis, and if this process continues such that the body is largely gaining its energy supply from ketones, the body enters a metabolic state known as ketosis [36].

By now, you may be thinking all of this keto talk sounds familiar, and you would be correct. Along with IF, the ketogenic or 'keto' diet is currently, wildly popular although the diet's use is similarly centuries-old, dating back to the treatment of epilepsy in 50 B.C. [37] [38]. The point of the keto diet is to purposely induce a state of ketosis in the body by restricting sugar and carbohydrate consumption to such a point that the body uses ketones as its source of energy [39]. Although it should be practiced with caution and is not meant to be a long-term way of life because it can lead to ketoacidosis which is deadly, ketosis has been linked to a host of health benefits in addition to the treatment of epilepsy. These benefits include the treatment of cancer [39], heart disease [40], and Parkinson's disease along with other neurodegenerative conditions [41].

Now that we are all experts in autophagy and ketosis, let's move on to another theory scientists have studied in determining why IF is so beneficial. This third theory is much simpler and somewhat obvious: IF contributes to an inherent reduction of overall calorie intake [14]. Reducing calories is imperative because we live in a society accustomed to eating all day long. It is completely reasonable, in an average day, to eat 3 large meals with snacks ranging from healthy to atrocious tucked between those meals at all hours of the day. Eating has become such a mindless task that people forget what all they have consumed in a day, leading to consuming substantially more calories than they realize.

There is such a large body of evidence demonstrating the prevalence of people who underestimate their caloric intake that it would take up the entirety of this book. This is not just an "American thing", either; research performed in many different countries demonstrates underestimation of calorie estimation is a common issue. For example, in early 2018 the United Kingdom (U.K.) Office of National Statistics released data showing 1/3 of U.K. adults underestimated their calorie consumption [42]. The chief nutritionist of Public Health England stated this underestimation is common because people often forget what they have eaten throughout the day. And, some respondents may change their answers on the food intake survey, claiming they eat less than they actually do to be more socially acceptable [42].

Given how prevalent the underestimation of calorie intake is, IF serves as sort of a natural solution to this because it limits the number of meals consumed per day. With fewer meals, the likelihood of forgetting what has been eaten drops dramatically [14]. Furthermore, the length of the fasting period only leaves a certain number of hours for calorie consumption. So not only meals are reduced, but the number of hours eating is reduced, making it inherently easier to keep track of intake. This is beneficial because reducing calorie intake over time may lead to weight loss, rolling over to improved health outcomes like reduced risk of cancers and obesity-related diseases [14] [37]. Perhaps obvious, but these health benefits of IF related to weight loss may be diminished if overconsumption takes place during nonfasting periods leading to either no weight loss or weight gain [14].

The Physical Benefits Of Fasting

Before I dig into the next sections, let me clear up some potentially confusing terminology. When I refer to chronic disease, it means disease that cannot be passed from one person to another, and it develops over a (sometimes long) period of time. Infectious disease, on the other hand, is acute disease that you can acquire from someone else like the flu or the common cold and typically resides after treatment. Because chronic disease develops over time, risk factors are things like poor diet, sedentarism, obesity, smoking, high blood pressure (hypertension), and drinking alcohol that can increase the chance someone develops a chronic disease [43]. This is important because research has associated IF with improvement in *chronic disease* and relevant risk factors, and this is what I will be referring to over the course of the following sections.

The majority of research on the physical benefits of IF to-date has been on animals (i.e., rodents) rather than humans, but the results are still promising [14]. In rodents, IF has been linked to prolonged life [14] and protection against cardiovascular disease, hypertension, insulin insensitivity, obesity, neuronal damage, and cancer [34] [35]. You may wonder what the deal is with using rodents, and what I will tell you is rodents have similar genetics, biology, and behaviors to humans; well, similar enough that they can be used as proxies for humans when it is not scientifically feasible to test humans. Especially in nutrition studies, it is difficult to recruit people, and it is also difficult to control for all of the confounding factors humans possess including factors that interfere with metabolism and underlying diseases. This is all beyond the scope of this book, but just know that using rodents in scientific research is common and the specific reason or reasons for the IF benefits seen in rodents are not entirely understood. As I go through each benefit and explain a little more in depth, I will add what scientists speculate thus far based on the most current research.

Don't get too excited because this is not a bookselling anti-aging propaganda, but research has shown IF to prolong life in rodents. In fact, research suggests that long-term dietary restriction is the only proven mechanism of prolonging life in rodents, worms, yeast, and flies [44]. Why this happens is not entirely understood, but speculation is that dietary restriction leads to reduction in oxidative damage in cells, altered neuroendocrine signaling which has to do with the brain-hormone relationship, and improved insulin sensitivity [44]. Alternate-day fasting as a proxy for long-term dietary restriction produces similar, life-prolonging qualities in rodents [45]. And, these benefits were intact even when the fasting rodents were the same weight and received the same energy intake as rodents who ate at their free will meaning the fasting benefits were independent of other health indicators [45].

Historically, heart disease, stroke, diabetes, and some cancers were only major issues in high-income countries due to a host of reasons including mass consumption of unhealthy and processed foods, as well as environmental and lifestyle stressors to name a few [46]. However, in recent decades, these chronic diseases have become major contributors to disease and death worldwide [46]. This change is not due to natural changes in the environment; rather, this change is near completely attributed to worsening behaviors associated with diet and lifestyle habits [46].

Cardiovascular disease has been the number one cause of death in the United States (U.S.) and one of the primary causes of death worldwide for decades [47]. The risk factors for cardiovascular disease include high cholesterol, hypertension, smoking cigarettes, overweight and obesity, poor diet, and drinking alcohol [47]. You may notice what all of these risk factors have in common: each one of them is directly linked to or literally is our diet and lifestyle. And, as you see, some of the risk factors go hand-in-hand in a sort of cyclical cause-and-effect cycle. For example, hypertension and obesity are both risk factors for cardiovascular disease, but obesity is also a risk factor for hypertension. Obesity is also a risk factor for insulin insensitivity, cancer, and neuronal damage, all of these, if you recall, are health indicators that IF has been shown to improve [48]. This makes sense because IF contributes to weight loss and often to healthier eating patterns that combat some of the risk factors associated with chronic disease [48].

While, as I already mentioned, the majority of research has been performed on rodents, there is human subject research as well it is just not as abundant. As a scientific researcher myself, I will tell you nutrition-based studies are difficult, expensive, and sometimes unreliable because of issues with participant self-report and confounding factors that can bias the results. So far, human subject research has linked IF to weight loss [49] and improvement in disease biomarkers related to cancer, cardiovascular disease, and diabetes [34] [50]. The same speculation for why these disease biomarker improvements due to IF exist in rodents has been speculated for humans.

Weight loss is a different IF outcome that has been measured extensively in humans with quite impressive results [7] [8]. One systematic review and meta-analysis of IF studies (think: the culmination of all the existing research on IF) found that overweight, adult participants lost an average of 15 pounds over the course of 3 months to a year depending on the form of IF being practiced [14]. Yet another review of IF literature on overweight or obese adults found that IF led to a 3-8% reduction in starting body weight over the course of 3-24 weeks [14]. Waist circumference was also reduced in the latter study, which is good news because midsection adiposity (i.e., belly fat) is linked to a host of cardiovascular issues [14].

You might notice how both of the reviews cited included extremely short-term results. This is because there have yet to be any long-term scientific research studies on IF and weight loss in humans. You may also notice that the result windows, for example, 3 months to 1 year, are quite wide. With the limited studies that are available, not only are they short-term but they vary on the timeframe during which the participants were subjected to IF. And finally, you may notice that no one IF method was chosen to be reviewed in either of the studies; rather, both reviews incorporated a vast array of different IF types and synthesized their weight loss outcomes. With so few human IF studies in existence, especially those with as specific as an outcome of weight loss, the pickin's for studies to include were probably slim to none. I am telling you all of this to familiarize yourself with research and how to interpret these results. If you do not understand, you may see an average of 15 pounds lost within 3 months, which was likely seen in only one study, and then become disappointed after 3 months when you have not also lost 15 pounds.

Remember, you will see different weight loss results depending on the IF type you choose to follow, the diet and exercise plan you incorporate along with fasting, and most importantly: your individual body. Based on the research, you will likely see results if you stick to an IF plan over a period of time and monitor what you consume during nonfasting periods. And, aside from weight loss specifically, the take-home message of the research on the physical benefits of IF seems to be that practicing IF is good news in terms of better health, longer life, and disease prevention.

The Psychological Benefits Of Fasting

The psychological benefits of practicing IF are more good news, as research has found IF to promote brain health as well. Have you ever noticed how you feel sleepy after eating a big meal, but feel more alert when it has been some hours since you last ate? This is because during nutrient deprivation in mammals, while all other organs tend to decrease in size to preserve energy, the brain's size remains protected [39]. With the brain's size unscathed during periods of fasting, it is able to remain more active than while the body is in a satiated state directly after eating [15].

To test this theory, researchers performed a series of psychological tests on rodents they subjected to IF. The results suggested that practicing IF led to increased performance on behavioral tests related to sensory and motor function, as well as learning and memory [37]. The researchers explained how the rodents' increased performance on the psychological tests after practicing IF were because of enhanced production of neurons and increased synaptic plasticity in the brain [37]. In simple terms, fasting accelerated the brain activity of the rodents and improved their cognitive ability to perform behavioral tests. While this has never been studied in humans, the suggestion would be that practicing IF would lead to improved cognitive (read: brain) function in terms of information retention and memory [37].

Aside from brain health in terms of cognitive function, IF has been linked to improved behavioral and mental health as well [51]. A study at the University of Illinois-Chicago was performed in response to skeptics claiming that alternate-day fasting or IF may lead to disordered eating patterns and negative body image [51]. This study found that obese adults following an 8-week alternate-day fasting regimen reported lower disordered eating tendencies and improved body image after the 8 weeks were over [51]. The subject's improved body image could have been due to their inherent feeling better about their bodies after losing weight, not necessarily due to the diet itself. However, if this is the case, it still means that using IF as a mechanism for losing weight can lead to not only improved physical health but enhanced psychological well-being as well.

Diet While Fasting

Let's shift gears from the science and benefits of IF to putting IF into action. I promised in the first chapter of this book that we would talk about maintaining a healthy eating pattern while practicing IF to lose weight. For some of you, this will not mean changing much of your eating habits that you already have in place if you eat healthy most of the time and indulge once in a while. For others, this may mean substantially changing the way you eat to achieve the weight loss goals you have in mind. If you fit into the latter category, have no fear, we will get you on the right path.

One of the best attributes of IF is that it can easily fit into any lifestyle because you can structure the fasting periods around your routine [14]. This is especially true for your diet. If you know you like to eat during a certain time of day, and already have particular foods you desire during those times of day, then you are one step ahead in choosing which IF diet plan works best for you. For example, if you love breakfast, then you could begin fasting earlier the previous day or evening to fit breakfast into your diet and start the day off the way you prefer. Or, maybe you prefer to start eating at lunchtime and continue eating later on into the day. If this is the case, you would stop eating after dinner, however late that might be, and fast until lunch the following day.

After you specify which meals are most important to you, then start thinking about foods you would like to incorporate into your IF diet plan. Healthy eating does not necessarily mean restricted eating; there are plenty of healthy options to choose from at every meal of the day. Feel free to peruse the 10-day 16/8 sample plan in Chapter 2 of this book; you will see that, for every meal, you can eat healthy without sacrificing variety, taste, and convenience. If your goal is to lose weight, think about which fruits, vegetables and sources of protein you love to eat because these items will be staples in your IF meal plan. And remember, IF does not dictate what you eat, so the diet you choose to follow is not about forcing yourself to eat celery or broccoli for breakfast. The diet should be more about choosing healthy foods you know you will eat, such that you are able to maintain IF and make this a true lifestyle change.

Exercise While Fasting

As with maintenance of any healthy lifestyle, exercise is recommended (although not required) in addition to eating a balanced diet while practicing IF for weight loss [52]. Before beginning any new exercise routine, it is always recommended that you consult a doctor and understand what types of exercise are right for you. This is especially true for women practicing IF and especially for women new to exercise, IF, or both. Women's bodies are sensitive to long periods of fasting and exercise may exacerbate or worsen health outcomes like blood sugar control, hormone imbalance, and loss of bone density [14]. Use caution, and just like you took time in choosing the right IF plan, take time to consider which forms of exercise will be safe to practice while fasting based on your individual body.

In general, it is recommended to partake in moderate-intensity exercise between 30-60 minutes five days per week, or in high-intensity exercise between 20-60 minutes three days per week to maintain good health [53]. Modifications may need to be made to these recommendations during fasting depending on the individual, but overall exercising while fasting has been linked to quite positive results. Recall during the discussion of autophagy that exercise was one activity with the ability to activate the cellular process along with fasting [25]. A growing amount of research has shown that exercise also promotes ketosis by depleting glucose reservoirs.

Additionally, exercise while fasting has been associated with increased fat burning, glucose tolerance, and insulin insensitivity [39].

The type of exercise you choose to perform while practicing IF should ideally fit within your schedule, work well with the type of IF you are practicing, and help you achieve your health and/or weight loss goals. You may already have a certain fitness routine that you enjoy and already know works well for you; if this is the case, continue doing whatever this is. Be mindful of the fact that your body may respond differently to this routine while fasting if you have usually been partaking while satiated. If you find that your body, in fact, responds differently, for instance, you are no longer able to maintain the same level of intensity, this is okay. Simply adapt the routine such that you reduce the intensity enough to finish the workout in the beginning and you will likely be able to build back up to the higher intensity over time.

Aside from the women with an already-established exercise regimen are those who are new to exercise, whether they have never found their groove before or it has been a long time since exercise has been a part of their life. The good news is: you don't have to be a bodybuilder or Crossfit expert to lose weight on IF. Choose a form of exercise that you know you can fit in on a normal day, and you think would be realistic to sustain over time. For example, if you think group exercise classes might work best for your schedule because they occur at a set time each day, but you know group exercise classes are not your thing, don't choose this. Something as simple as a 30-minute jog, walk, or bicycle ride most days of the week would be fine if that is what you like to do. Only you know best what will jive with your work schedule, what you will want to stick with, and what will get you where you want to be health- and/or weight-wise.

Still speaking to beginners: after choosing the exercise that works best for you, which keep in mind might change and adapt over the course of your IF journey, ease into it. It is not a good idea to embark on a drastic fasting routine *and* an intense new workout routine at the same time. This is a recipe for giving up after a week, and giving up will not get you to the weight or health status you want to be. If it has been an extraordinarily long time since you have exercised, start with 15-minute exercise increments and work your way up over time. Sneak in steps by parking farther away from the office, store, or other destination than you usually would. Take the stairs! You have likely heard all these tricks somewhere before and let me tell you, they add up. Before you know it, your workouts will be 30 minutes long, then an hour-long, and you will be amazed at your progress in a short amount of time.

For beginners and exercise enthusiasts alike, the thought and perhaps the actual act of working out on an empty stomach may seem excruciating. It does not have to be excruciating, though, if you plan ahead and change your mindset. For example, if you choose the 16/8 Method of IF, think about how you would normally work out after you wake up from sleeping for 7-8 hours. Although not purposefully fasting, you are actually fasting during this time period. If you typically workout first thing in the morning, your exercise during IF will not be substantially different if your 16-hour fasting period is largely while you are sleeping. What *will* be different is how you recover after the workout if you are accustomed to eating breakfast when you are finished. A couple of different options would be to begin fasting earlier the evening before so that you are able to eat breakfast as normal after your workout in the morning. Or, if fasting extends well beyond your workout and you know that you will not be able to maintain not eating breakfast afterward, consider fitting your workout in during a different time of day.

Intermittent Fasting Hacks

We all know how difficult sticking to a diet regimen long-term can be. A common phrase throughout IF literature is that the practice should become a "lifestyle" change, as opposed to a diet. While it sounds cliché and perhaps a little silly, garnering this mindset of IF becoming a way of life rather than a short-term fix is a fundamental first step in maintaining the practice [54]. Keep in mind that IF is not only for weight loss, but for a host of healthy rewards like longevity, disease prevention, and improved cognitive function. Stay mindful of the changes your body goes through as time passes and adjust the type of IF being practiced as needed rather than giving up on it altogether.

Even with the foundation of a healthy mindset in place, fasting days may still be challenging. This is especially true in the initial days of adopting IF when the body is adjusting to a new regimen. Most types of IF allow water and black coffee to be consumed during fasting days; take advantage of these beverages [55][56]. While too much caffeine can lead to dehydration and fatigue, consuming one cup of coffee in the morning and/or one cup in the afternoon to maintain energy may help combat the urge to indulge while tired and low in motivation. Water, on the other hand, should be a staple throughout the day, not only to stay hydrated but to improve energy, focus, metabolism, and to help feel full [55]. If plain water is not your thing and the thought of drinking water all day is excruciating, add some flavor to your water. This day-in-age there are plenty of options for flavor additions, but you may also consider filling a large pitcher with ice water and adding cut-up fruit like strawberries and citrus into the water for natural flavor.

While fasting, avoid sitting around thinking about fasting [56]. This might seem obvious, but it is easy to dread the fasting period, then think about how dreadful the fasting period is while you are in it. Try to keep yourself busy by taking walks or bike rides, getting out of the house to enjoy a park or venue of interest, losing yourself in a novel, or partaking in any activities you find enjoyable. If the fasting period falls during the time you are working, perhaps take breaks when permitted to walk around the office or building, find a project to stay engaged in, or listen to a podcast while you work if possible. Be sure to keep your water bottle full throughout the day and allow yourself a boost with black coffee or tea when needed.

Especially when following the IF types where fasting lasts 14-16 hours, use the time you are sleeping as part of the fasting period [56]. After finishing dinner, stop eating and start fasting! If you stop eating by 7-8 pm, the majority of the fasting period will be the time directly prior to sleeping, sleeping, and the initial waking up in the morning. Drink a large glass of water and grab a cup of black coffee instead of breakfast; before you know it, the fast is over just in time to enjoy lunch. For those of you trying longer fasting periods like the Eat Stop Eat Method, structure the long fasting days around work or other activities you know will make fasting more difficult [56]. For instance, if you know Wednesdays or a particular day is always longer than the others, do not fast on Wednesdays or a longer particular day. Try to choose a calm or an otherwise less busy day to fast so that you are able to distract yourself freely with walks, music, podcasts, movies, and the like. Pro tip: you will be thankful for having an open bathroom all day between the fast and water consumption, too.

During nonfasting periods, eat small meals and snacks spread evenly throughout the day or evening, depending on the IF structure you choose. Eating several small meals and snacks as opposed to one or two big meals spread far apart will help maintain blood sugar levels and will more importantly stave off hunger [57]. Especially if you structure nonfasting periods during the workday, bring healthy snacks with you to munch on throughout the day and during breaks to avoid crashing or feeling starved. Choose small meals and snacks high in protein, fiber, or both to ensure you feel satiated longer [56].

Implement ways to control your stress levels during IF [55][58]. Stress can lead to overeating and otherwise unhealthy habits that could completely derail any of the benefits of fasting. Everyone's life is busy these days, but you must find a few moments of downtime each day to focus on stress relief. This will look different for different people, but some common tactics include yoga, meditation, stretching, mindfulness practice, spending time in nature, and exercise. Whatever method works best for you makes no difference; what matters most is that you take the time to practice this daily or regularly to avoid falling into stress-ridden setbacks in your health and weight loss journey.

Apple cider vinegar (ACV) is one of my most favorite personal health hacks of all time. It is a versatile cooking ingredient that packs a punch with health benefits, including lowering blood sugar and increasing fat loss [59]. The reason why I love ACV so much is that it balances Ph levels in your body which can help combat yeast infections, acne, and a host of inflammation-related conditions [59]. Concerning IF, this hack has been touted to reduce hunger by equalizing the bad bacteria in your gut [59]. How you choose to consume ACV is up to you and will produce the same benefits regardless of the method. However, let me warn you: this stuff is potent. Do not just pour it into a shot glass and take it like a shot unless you have a throat of steel. While many people do this to 'get it out of the way' and move on with their day, I have tried this method and literally thought I permanently damaged my throat because it burned so severely on the way down. I would highly recommend adding ACV to a salad dressing or diluting 1 or 2 teaspoons of it into a glass of water.

Weight Loss Hacks

While the benefits of IF are not limited to weight loss, this may be the most common reason why most people (including women) become interested in practicing IF. As already mentioned, because IF inherently reduces the frequency of meals being eaten and may reduce overall caloric intake, the odds are favorable that people will lose weight while practicing IF. However, because IF does not dictate a specific diet regimen, there are ways to increase the odds of weight loss by going a little further than simply fasting and incorporating other healthy lifestyle habits.

The biggest trick to achieving weight loss during IF is to stay mindful of eating healthy meals while nonfasting [56]. Fasting is not magic; just because you have fasted for several hours to a full day, this does not mean you can otherwise consume calories uncontrollably and still lose weight. If you are following a plan that allows consumption up to a certain caloric range on a fasting day (think, the 5:2 Method), make the calories count. Stick with foods that are high in protein and fiber, like chicken or beef, green leafy vegetables, and low-carbohydrate fruits like green apples that do not singularly add many calories to the total allotment for the day. This way, you will *feel* like you are eating more, but the actual calories being consumed are kept at bay. On nonfasting days, especially when weight loss is the goal, consumption should still consist largely of nutrient-rich options like fruits and vegetables, nuts and seeds, protein, healthy carbohydrates like brown rice, and low-sugar dairy.

In addition to healthy caloric consumption during fasting and nonfasting periods, exercise is key to achieving weight loss during IF. In general, being active is critical for maintaining optimal health and disease prevention; during IF the importance of exercise is no different [56]. Because women tend to be more sensitive to the effects of IF versus men, it is also recommended that exercise during IF is within reasonable limits of what each woman can tolerate. For some women, taking a brisk walk might be the highest level of exercise recommended during IF. Yet other women may tolerate higher-intensity cardio or weight lifting during IF. Furthermore, the mode and/or intensity of exercise may change over time as the body adjusts to IF. The most important thing is to choose the method of exercise that best fits your individual needs.

For weight loss, in particular, be wary of which zero-calorie beverages you choose [55]. This may sound bizarre because it would be easy to assume zero-calorie anything could never lead to weight loss. However, research has shown mixed results on whether sugar-free products like diet soda and flavored water that often contain artificial sugars like aspartame actually stimulate appetite due to their effect on the brain [60]. Naturally, although the beverage itself has zero calories, this effect has been linked to weight gain in some studies because people ended up overeating [60]. In other, more recent, studies this effect of artificial sweeteners stimulating appetite to the point of overconsumption is not true, completely negating what the previous research showed [61]. As I said, dieting is hard. To avoid confusion and the potential that the earlier research is, in fact, true for you, look for zero-calorie beverages that do not contain artificial sweeteners by reading the package nutrition label thoroughly.

We all know to brush our teeth after every meal or at least twice per day for optimal dental hygiene. But, brushing teeth has been long believed to help reduce hunger, too [62]. This is due to the flavor of mint being linked to suppressing appetite. And, since most toothpaste is mint flavored, alas, the connection [62]. Mint flavored sugar-free chewing gum is also suggested being that brushing your teeth all day long is not exactly recommended. Also not recommended is chewing too much sugar-free gum because of the discussion above on artificial sugars, and because sugar alcohols can lead to diarrhea and general gastrointestinal discomfort when consumed in excess [62].

Furthermore, the research has been mixed on whether either method actually works for hunger suppression. While in one study, gum-chewing participants consumed fewer calories and burned 5% more calories throughout the day compared to non-gum-chewers [62], other research demonstrated no effect of gum chewing on weight loss or managing hunger [62]. All in all, chewing gum or brushing your teeth may be simple ways to keep your mind off of fasting and help you push through particularly difficult fasting days. And your breath will smell fantastic!

Sleep is unbelievably underappreciated when it comes to health and weight loss. Nowadays, our culture is wired to nonstop information and the use of electronic devices that interfere with both the amount of sleep we get each night and the quality of sleep received when we do manage to sleep [63]. Research shows this essential sleep deprivation that the majority of the population is suffering from actually increases the risk of obesity by affecting appetite, metabolism, motivation, and level of physical activity [64]. The short of it: you need sleep. And, you likely need more sleep than you think you do. Aim for 7-8 hours of sleep per night and avoid screen time on your phone, television, laptop, and other electronic devices at least an hour before you turn out the lights as these devices can interfere with your ability to fall asleep.

For weight loss, another *zero* to stay mindful of aside from your zero-calorie beverages is your intake during fasting [65]. True fasting means *zero* calorie intake, and this may seem obvious, but it is necessary to point out because calories have a tendency to be sneaky. For instance, if you are a regular coffee drinker, ask yourself what you put in your coffee this morning. Did you add cream, milk, and/or sugar? And, did you forget you added these items until I just asked you? During your fasting periods, these items would technically not be suggested because they do in fact have calories. This is why I have been mindful to state "black coffee" specifically throughout this book as an encouraging beverage during fasting periods including water and other zero-calorie beverages.

I am going to break protocol and keep talking about sneaky calories in this paragraph because I feel as though many of you may have just realized you cannot live without coffee creamer and are seeing stars. This goes for tea and other beverages that you may not have until-now realized you have been adding calories to as well. First of all: *don't worry.* Adding a teaspoon of creamer to your coffee or sweetener to your tea during fasting periods will not throw off your entire weight loss plan. However, there are some things you can do to avoid these hidden calories from adding up. My first tip is to reduce the amount of cream, milk, and/or sugar you normally add until eventually the ingredients are excluded altogether. Or, if black coffee and/or plain tea are just not realistic for you, my second tip is to either substantially reduce the number of extras you are adding or to substitute whatever it is that you are adding with something low- or zero-calorie. While it is important you are not consuming calories during the fasting period, even more important is that IF fits into your lifestyle as you are so that it is sustainable.

Okay, now that we have avoided the hidden calorie crisis, let's talk about your schedule. A simple but extremely useful hack to achieve weight loss while practicing IF is to keep your schedule consistent [65]. Once you nail down the IF plan that fits best for you, try it out for a few weeks and try to keep the schedule somewhat regular from day-to-day. For example, if you fast between 8 pm-12 pm, try to eat lunch, snacks, and dinner at the same time each day.

Additionally, try to work out, fit in your walks, or whatever type of activity you plan to do around the same time each day as well. This not only helps you plan ahead by having your meals prepared and your workout clothes ready to go, but it also keeps your body on somewhat of a routine. This is to say, you may notice after a few weeks that your body naturally becomes hungry around Noon, feels antsy in the afternoon right before your workout, and becomes hungry again around the time you normally eat dinner. Of course, you will have the impromptu dinner plans and whatnot that spring up for all of us, and you will simply work around these unanticipated plans as you normally would; however, there is a lot to be said about consistency when maintaining a long-term lifestyle change.

Right when you got used to the idea of consistency, I am going to throw you a curveball: if you notice your body hitting a plateau, change things up [65]. This does not necessarily mean throwing your entire consistency plan out the window, but it does mean to listen to your body and make sure you continue seeing results over time. If you follow the same IF plan for 6 months or a year and notice yourself feeling bored or those last pounds are not seeming to budge, don't be afraid to tweak your plan. For instance, if you have been following the 16/8 Method for a long time, maybe throw in a 24-hour fast on a day that you know you could swing it. After the 24-hour fast, consume calories until you would normally begin your 16-hour fast and get right back into business as usual. Or, if the change needs to be more drastic, consider changing to a different IF plan altogether that fits your needs better now compared to when you started.

Common Pitfalls And How To Avoid Them

Perhaps the most common pitfall in practicing IF is giving up too soon [66]. This is where adapting the "lifestyle change" mindset matters most. While fasting has been practiced since the beginning of time, it is not easy. Especially in a culture where food is not only always available but is essentially consumed at all hours of the day. It will take time for the body to adjust to such a drastically different lifestyle change. Remember, you can always modify or change the type of IF being practiced to best fit your individual needs. If fasting for 24 hours straight is not realistic for your lifestyle, perhaps consider trying a type of IF where the majority of time fasting is spent sleeping. Or, a type of IF where the fasts do not last so long.

Similar to giving up too soon is having unrealistic expectations of the results IF will produce [55]. Unrealistic expectations might include both how drastic the results will be and how quickly these results are achieved. As previously mentioned, the benefits of IF are not limited to weight loss or other visible, short-term results like inches lost from the waistline. Many of the benefits gleaned from IF may not be physically felt (i.e., prevention of cancer, diabetes, and cardiovascular disease) and these results may not occur until IF has been practiced for some time. Additionally, results may be tied to the type of IF being practiced and how strict the IF plan is being followed. To avoid the pitfall of having unrealistic expectations, review your goals before you begin IF. Losing 30 pounds in one month may not be realistic; however, losing 8 pounds and feeling more energized may serve as achievable goals.

Attempting too much too soon is another pitfall with IF that should be avoided [66]. Especially for women, modified versions of IF are recommended to ensure that injury or harm is avoided. No one should be jumping into a 24 hour fast on the first day of IF.

Before you begin any type of IF, take time to educate yourself by reading through the different types, compare the pros and cons of each, and most importantly speak with your doctor about your plan. Fasting, when done properly, should not lead to starvation or dangerous levels of nutrient deprivation that could spur serious, negative health outcomes. Choose the type of IF that fits your individual metabolism, caloric needs, and lifestyle rather than the type of IF that you feel will bring the most rapid results.

Overeating on nonfasting days may mitigate some of the benefits of IF and is a common pitfall because, well, after fasting for several hours you may want to eat the first thing that crosses your path [66]. Even though IF does not require a specific diet plan, it is still recommended to follow a healthy eating pattern the majority of time with sporadic indulgence. To avoid the pitfall of overeating or overindulging in unhealthy foods during nonfasting periods, prepare meals ahead of time. Especially the first meal after fasting, having something quick, healthy, and already prepared may help prevent reaching for something less nutritious out of desperation. If you find yourself a poor chef or need assistance thinking about different food options, look no further! In an upcoming chapter, we will go over a 10-day meal plan for the 16/8 Method that you can steal shamelessly and adapt to your particular taste.

Avoid the break room at all costs, if you know your co-workers are notorious for bringing in goodies to share with the office. In fact, when reasonable, avoid places you know will serve as a temptation to stray from fasting on fasting days and to consume high-calorie, low-nutrient foods on nonfasting days. Sources of temptation are often restaurants, businesses that serve high-calorie caffeinated beverages, bakeries and processed foods in grocery stores, keeping unhealthy snacks in the pantry at home, and potluck style parties and get-togethers.

Because it is not always possible to avoid every temptation, keep healthy snacks within reach on nonfasting days and keep a full water bottle on-hand on fasting days to help.

Choosing the wrong type of IF for your individual body and lifestyle needs is nearly guaranteed to set yourself up for failure from the get-go [66]. It has been reiterated throughout this book and will continue to be, but it is absolutely imperative that the IF plan you follow not only fits the more complicated things like your metabolism, hormonal, and caloric needs, but also fits the simpler things like your work schedule. Do you work a 9 am to 5 pm job? Or, do you work the overnight shift? Do you tend to work on weekends? And how many hours per week do you work? These may all seem like trivial factors but are actually fundamental in whether the IF plan you choose is going to be sustainable or not. For instance, you probably do not want to be fasting for 16 hours while you are working if you work overnights and have a fast-paced job. Avoid this pitfall by truly adapting your IF plan to your life. If you work overnights, your "lunch" may be at Midnight instead of Noon, meaning you may need to fast during the day instead.

The last pitfall we are going to talk about is extremely common, but you may not even realize you are doing it: confusing appetite with hunger. These two words do not mean the same thing. Appetite refers to the *desire* to eat and has everything to do with the brain-gut connection [67]. When you see your favorite food, whether chocolate chip cookies or a savory plate of comfort food, your mouth may begin to water. This is the brain telling your belly "that food looks delicious," and this elicits an actual, physical response that is actually tied to the emotion of desire toward the food. Hunger, on the other hand, refers to the *need* to eat [66]. Hunger cannot be controlled and is not elicited by an emotional brain-gut response to desirable food; rather, hunger is an actual, primal response to the body needing energy to survive. Your body signals actual hunger through stomach pangs, stomach rumblings, and a drop in blood sugar that can lead to other health symptoms [67]. In other words, appetite is our *want* to eat, while hunger is our *need* to eat. Avoiding this pitfall means you may need to do some work in learning your body's signals and understanding the difference in your body when it is hungry versus when you have an appetite. Another helpful practice is to drink a glass of water when you think you feel hungry because you may actually be thirsty rather than hungry.

How To Get Started

Meal Sizing

Before beginning an IF meal plan, it is imperative to take time reading about the unique nutritional requirements to maintain optimal health. This is especially true for women, who may need different types and amounts of nutrients due to their individual body's needs. For instance, women with longer or heavier periods may require higher iron intake even when they are not practicing IF; thus, because fasting will deplete iron levels, and this can lead to negative health outcomes, these women may need to consider meals with larger amounts of animal protein, green leafy vegetables, and various types of beans [68].

With precautions out of the way, let's talk about meal sizing and spacing while you are practicing IF. Since we are about to go into a detailed 10-day sample plan for the 16/8 Method, I will use this method as an example. It is up to you when you plan to fast for 16 hours (12-14 hours in the beginning) and eat during the remaining hours of the day. However, regardless of when you plan to eat, it is recommended that you space your eating evenly across several small meals and snacks throughout the day to keep your blood sugar in check [69]. This will also keep hunger at bay, especially if you choose snacks and meals high in protein and fiber.

A wonderful advantage of IF is that no calorie-counting is required unless you choose a plan like the 5:2 Method that restricts calorie intake to a specific amount during fasting periods [14]. It would still be wise, though, to avoid overconsumption or obvious snacks (i.e., doughnuts) when weight loss is a goal. If you are wondering how it is possible to avoid overconsumption without counting calories, my recommendation is to focus on filling your plate with a wide variety of colorful, whole foods and savoring your meals rather than wolfing them down. Colorful, whole foods like vegetables and fruits are naturally low in calories, high in fiber, and also high in water content such that you feel full while consuming less.

Savoring your meals is also pertinent to *allowing* yourself to feel full. It takes 20 minutes for our brain to register the chemicals released when our body reaches the point of fullness; we often eat so much so fast that by the time this occurs, we have already overconsumed [70]. Drink plenty of water with your meal and wait 15 to 20 minutes after your first plate to decide whether you truly need more. If you have always inhaled your food and slowing down your eating seems like a difficult task, there are a couple of tricks that have helped me.

The first trick is to avoid eating while you multitask; rather, when you eat a meal, focus only on eating that meal and be mindful of the way you feel while eating. Sit at a dining table or other sort of table that is only designed for eating, without your phone, computer, television, or other distractions nearby. This will force you to focus on how much food you are consuming and monitor your hunger level while you are consuming it. Often what happens when we eat while working, watching television, playing on our phones, and so on is that we are so distracted that we don't realize how much we are eating nor when we've become full.

Along with being focused on eating, the second trick is to physically slow down your eating [70]. This may involve literally chewing slower or chewing more per bite than you normally do. Sometimes what helps me is to chew to the tune of a song. For example, for every bite you take, sing happy birthday in your head and make sure you keep chewing until the song ends before you take another bite and repeat. Don't worry, you won't have to do this forever. Once you are used to slower eating and/or chewing more per bite, it will become second-nature without needing the song or extra concentration.

Another thing to keep in mind regarding meal sizing and calorie consumption is not to allow what those around you eat to influence what you eat [71]. It may be inevitable that you eat some of your daily meals with your family, friends, co-workers, roommates, or others depending on your individual circumstances. This is where food envy may creep in, and this is also where your defenses may be lowered because you think to yourself, if *that* person is eating *that* food or *that much* of *that* food, then maybe it won't be a big deal if I do too. While you may not be able to avoid these situations, you can control how you react to these situations. Try to focus on how good you feel when you eat healthy foods and when you stop eating after your body signals you are full. Also, remember how good it feels to fit into those jeans you have been dying to wear but could not fit into before you made all of these lifestyle changes! And, most importantly, remember that each of these meals is temporary while the health benefits of staying on track are long-term. You will likely forget that meal, but you won't forget how good you feel for the rest of your life.

10 Day Sample Routine

16/8 Method

For the first 4 days of the 16/8 Method, start out by fasting for 12-14 hours before working up to fasting for 16 hours. The night before day 1 of practicing IF, stop eating at 8 pm.

*Snacks: Listen to your body. If you are so hungry that you feel dizzy, weak, or fatigued, eat a snack. Be sure to drink water throughout the day as you could confuse thirst with hunger.

Day 1: Start Eating At 8 AM

8 am Breakfast – Low-sugar yogurt, 1 cup of oatmeal topped with cinnamon and blueberries, 8 oz of water, 1 cup black coffee (optional).

Brush your teeth before you go to work.

10-11 am *Snack – 1 ~200 calorie protein bar, 8 oz of water.

If possible, take a break at work to walk for 15 minutes or stretch next to your desk to increase blood flow and relaxation.

12 pm Lunch – Salad with spinach, mixed vegetables, chicken, and cut-up tangerines or berries of choice. 8 oz of water.

Stay mindful of your body during this time. If you cannot wait until 3 or 4 pm to have a snack because you feel light-headed or too hungry to focus, eat your snack, and do 10 jumping jacks next to your desk if possible.

Brush your teeth or chew a piece of mint-flavored sugar-free gum if you chew gum and need an extra distraction.

3-4 pm *Snack – Handful of grapes, cheese, and crackers, 8 oz of water, 1 cup of black coffee (optional).

Before or after dinner, exercise as normal. Or, if you are just starting an exercise regimen along with your IF plan, start slow with walking or riding a bicycle for 30 minutes.

7-8 pm Dinner – Grilled chicken or beef, side vegetable of choice, and brown rice or quinoa. 8 oz of water.

After dinner – only water consumption until bed. Eat a snack if you feel so hungry you will not be able to sleep.

Day 2: Start Eating At 9 AM

Brush your teeth before you go to work.

9 am Breakfast – 1 medium banana, 1 bowl of high-fiber cereal with skim milk, 8 oz of water, and 1 cup black coffee (optional).

10-11 am *Snack – 1 ~200 calorie protein shake, 8 oz of water.

Get up and stretch next to your desk if possible, do 10 jumping jacks, or take a brisk walk around the building.

12 pm Lunch – Turkey burger topped with lettuce, tomato, and pickles or another desired vegetable combination. 1 handful of plantain chips, 8 oz of water.

If possible, take another break to get your blood flowing and occupy your mind. If you cannot take another break or leave your desk but can listen to music or a podcast, choose something that you enjoy listening to while you work.

Brush your teeth or chew a piece of mint-flavored sugar-free gum.

3-4 pm *Snack – Green apple slices with almond butter dip, 8 oz of water, 1 cup of black coffee (optional).

Stretch before or after dinner for 30 minutes while watching your favorite TV show, book, or other form of entertainment.

7-8 pm Dinner – Grilled salmon, side green vegetable of choice, and mashed sweet potatoes. 8 oz of water.

After dinner – only water consumption until bed. Eat a snack if you feel so hungry you will not be able to sleep.

Day 3: Start Eating At 9 AM

Brush your teeth before you go to work.

9 am Breakfast – 1 handful of strawberries, egg omelet with peppers and mushrooms or a desired vegetable combination, 2 slices of whole wheat toast, 8 oz of water, and 1 cup black coffee (optional).

10-11 am *Snack – Greek yogurt (low-sugar fruit flavored or plain topped with berries), 8 oz of water.

Using your desk as a base, do 10 slow push-ups to get your body moving and blood flowing.

12 pm Lunch – Greek salad with grilled chicken, romaine lettuce, olives, banana peppers and feta cheese, 8 oz of water.

Walk to the furthest water fountain to refill your water bottle, or take a lap around the office, saying hello to co-workers to get your body moving and keep your mind active.

Brush your teeth or chew a piece of mint-flavored sugar-free gum.

3-4 pm *Snack – Celery and carrots with ranch dressing, 1 handful of pita chips, 8 oz of water, 1 cup of black coffee (optional).

Before or after dinner, do your normal exercise routine or find a 30 minutes workout video to follow online if you are a beginner. Try to find a video that targets your goal, whether it be firmer arms or abs, a stronger core, or longer endurance.

7-8 pm Dinner – Grilled steak, sweet corn on the cob, and baked red potatoes. 8 oz of water.

After dinner – only water consumption until bed. Eat a snack if you feel so hungry you will not be able to sleep.

Day 4: Start Eating At 10 AM

Although you start eating food at 10 am today, start drinking water as soon as you wake up to kickstart your metabolism and get your body fluids flowing. It is also okay to drink black coffee or another zero-calorie beverage of your choice during this time.

Brush your teeth before you go to work.

10 am Breakfast – 1 orange, 2 whole wheat pancakes topped with blueberries and agave, 8 oz of water, and 1 cup black coffee (optional).

Without a snack, you may feel anxious for lunch to arrive. Stay occupied by taking a break at work if you can to stretch, do jumping jacks, or take a quick walk.

12 pm Lunch – Salad with beef tips, spinach, mixed vegetables, quinoa, and 8 oz of water.

Chew a piece of mint-flavored sugar-free gum. Or, brush your teeth if you can.

3-4 pm *Snack – ~200 calorie protein bar or shake, 8 oz of water, 1 cup of black coffee (optional).

Before or after dinner, practice stretching or yoga for 30 minutes.

7-8 pm Dinner – Smothered baked chicken with marinara sauce and peppers, green vegetable of choice, whole grain pasta, and 8 oz of water.

After dinner – only water consumption until bed. Eat a snack if you feel so hungry you will not be able to sleep.

Day 5: Start Eating At 12 PM

Again, without breakfast, make sure to drink water throughout the morning and black coffee as well as other zero-calorie beverages as needed. Since this is the first day you are doing the full-fast, do not feel ashamed if you cannot make it until 12 pm to eat. If you feel so hungry that you cannot focus at work, feel faint, or otherwise physically ill, eat a snack before lunch. Practice keeping your mind occupied by going for a brief walk or listening to your favorite music or podcast if/when you can.

As always, brush your teeth before work.

12 pm Lunch – Beef burger with whole grain bun topped with onions, lettuce, and tomato, baked sweet potato, and 8 oz of water.

Brush your teeth or chew one piece of mint-flavored sugar-free gum.

3-4 pm *Snack – Mixed nuts (cashews, almonds, pecans) with grapes and green apple slices, 1 cup of black coffee (optional).

If the area is safe, the restaurant is close enough, and you have a friend or partner along, walk instead of driving to the location. If you normally take public transit everywhere, get off at a stop a little further away and walk the rest of the distance. If walking is not possible and there is no time in between work and arriving for dinner, try to stretch after getting home from dinner or take the night to relax.

7-8 pm Dinner – Go out to eat at a sit-down restaurant. Order baked or grilled meat of choice, vegetable side like coleslaw, broccoli, or seasonal mixed vegetable, and a health grain or starch like potatoes, brown rice, quinoa, or whole grain pasta.

After dinner – only water consumption until bed. Eat a snack if you feel so hungry you will not be able to sleep.

Day 6: Start Eating At 12 PM

As with day 5, make sure to consume an abundance of water throughout the morning as well as black coffee and other zero-calorie beverages as needed. Also, as always, listen to your body. If you are too hungry before lunch to the point of feeling ill, eat a healthy snack beforehand.

Per usual, brush your teeth before work.

12 pm Lunch – Antipasto salad with whole grain pasta, tomatoes, spinach, olives, and chicken. 1 pear or fruit of choice and 8 oz of water.

If possible, take a break to walk for 15-20 minutes.

Brush your teeth or chew a piece of mint-flavored sugar-free gum.

3-4 pm *Snack – ~150 calorie protein bar or shake, 1 green apple, 1 cup of black coffee (optional).

Before or after dinner, perform normal exercise routine or continue targeting focus areas for 45 minutes if you are a beginner.

7-8 pm Dinner – Grilled fish, baked mixed vegetables like carrots, squash and zucchini, and broccoli, brown rice, and 8 oz of water.

After dinner – only water consumption until bed. Eat a snack if you feel so hungry you will not be able to sleep.

Day 7: Start Eating At 12 PM

This is the third day of full fasting for 16 hours: how are you feeling? Is there anything you want to change? What are you enjoying so far? Try to stay mindful of these things as you move forward to adjust your individual IF plan accordingly. Keep drinking plenty of water and zero-calorie beverages to stay hydrated and feeling full before lunch.

Brush your teeth before you go to work.

12 pm Lunch – Grilled chicken salad with spinach, olives, mixed peppers, and quinoa. 1 handful of pita chips with grapes and 8 oz of water.

Stretch, play music or a podcast, do push-ups or jumping jacks as you wish based on what has been working for you to stay occupied and active over the past several days.

Brush your teeth or chew one piece of mint-flavored sugar-free gum.

3-4 pm *Snack – 1 banana with peanut butter; if food allergy, pair fruit of choice with protein like cheese slices, Greek yogurt, or almond butter. 1 cup of black coffee (optional).

Did you know in most major cities there are free group exercise classes offered? If this is something you are interested in, try one tonight to change things up. However, if you are already attached to your fitness routine, or perhaps just need a break from all the exercise you have been doing as of late if this is new to you, go with what makes you happy. You get dessert tonight, after all!

7-8 pm Dinner – Steak, baked sweet potato, whole grain pasta with marinara sauce, and 8 oz of water. *Dessert of choice.*

After dinner – only water consumption until bed. Eat a snack if you feel so hungry you will not be able to sleep.

Day 8: Start Eating At 12 PM

You know the drill. Water galore and zero-calorie beverages before lunch. If you need to eat because you feel physically ill before lunch, choose a healthy snack, and make sure to get some fresh air with a walk.

Brush your teeth before you go to work

12 pm Lunch – Power bowl with black beans, sweet corn, mixed peppers, and quinoa or brown rice. 1 orange, and 8 oz of water.

Stretch at your desk or turn on music if you need a distraction.

Brush your teeth or chew one piece of mint-flavored sugar-free gum.

3-4 pm *Snack – 1 green apple, corn and celery sticks with ranch dressing dip, and 1 cup of black coffee (optional).

Before or after dinner, if you took last night off of exercise, resume working on your target area for 45 minutes.

7-8 pm Dinner – Baked chicken smothered with cream of mushroom or substitute desired creamy soup, steamed broccoli, and cornbread. 8 oz of water.

After dinner – only water consumption until bed. Eat a snack if you feel so hungry you will not be able to sleep.

Day 9: Start Eating At 12 PM

If you are getting bored already, switch things up. Although you still need to consume at least 8 glasses of water per day, the choices of non-zero beverages available these days is endless. Trying something new might be so exciting that you forget you are skipping breakfast!

Forget breakfast but do not forget to brush your teeth before you go to work.

12 pm Lunch – Turkey sandwich with whole-wheat bun, lettuce, and tomatoes. Mixed seasonal fruit like berries and 8 oz of water.

Take your snack for a walk today if you can and munch while you get your blood flowing.

When you get back from your potential walk, brush your teeth or chew one piece of mint-flavored sugar-free gum.

3-4 pm *Snack – Broccoli salad with grapes and 1 cup of black coffee (optional).

Before or after dinner, stretch or do a light yoga routine to wind down while still keeping your body active.

7-8 pm Dinner – Seafood of choice, green vegetable side like spinach or collard greens, and brown rice. 8 oz of water.

After dinner – only water consumption until bed. Eat a snack if you feel so hungry you will not be able to sleep.

Day 10: Start Eating At 12 PM

You have this. You have all the tricks up your sleeve by now to survive 10 days of IF; who says you have to stop here? Drink plenty of water and consume your favorite zero-calorie beverages until lunch.

Brush your teeth before you go to work.

12 pm Lunch – Chicken Caesar salad, whole grain bread, and 8 oz of water.

Do push-ups or jumping jacks at your desk if possible.

Brush your teeth or chew one piece of mint-flavored sugar-free gum.

3-4 pm *Snack – 1 handful of strawberries, carrots, and crackers with hummus and 1 cup of black coffee (optional).

Tonight, do your normal workout routine or if you are a beginner, keep working on your target areas for 30-45 minutes.

7-8 pm Dinner – Grilled kabobs with onion, peppers, mushrooms, and chicken over a bed of rice, quinoa, or other grain of choice. 8 oz of water.

After dinner – only water consumption until bed. Eat a snack if you feel so hungry you will not be able to sleep.

Side Effects Of Intermittent Fasting

The most obvious side effect of IF is hunger [72][73].

Common Side Effects of IF

- Hunger
- Headaches
- Low energy
- Overeating
- Bathroom breaks
- Coldness
- Hanger
- Cravings
- Heartburn/Bloating

If fasting is prolonged or hunger surpasses mild discomfort, this may interfere with sleep and clarity of mind, along with other health concerns. While these symptoms may be a result of the body adjusting to a new eating schedule, severe hunger or starvation may be a sign of something more serious, and it may be wise to eat a light snack and relax until the feelings pass. Before resuming the fast, be sure to consider whether the length of the fasting period is suitable or if increased calorie intake should occur during nonfasting periods to prevent the symptoms from happening again, or even worse injury or harm.

Dull headaches are another effect of IF [72] [73]. As with hunger, headaches may be a result of the body adjusting to fasting and may be short-term in nature. However, headaches may also be a signal that you are dehydrated. As it has been stressed throughout the entirety of this book: make sure you keep your water bottle within arms-length and keep drinking water all day long. Along with the obvious not drinking enough water, be aware that things you consume like caffeine and sodium can dehydrate you too. This means if you are a black coffee drinker, make sure to drink a glass of water per every cup of coffee you drink to maintain hydration.

Especially in the first couple of weeks of beginning an IF routine, you may feel weak, sluggish, or generally low in energy [72][73]. This is because your body is adjusting from normally receiving energy intake all day long to going extended periods without any energy intake at all. During this adjustment period, try not to stress about pushing yourself to the max during workouts and keep your daily routine fairly relaxed if possible. For those of you with office jobs, this will likely not be an issue. However, for those of you with more high-energy, quick-moving jobs, incorporate breaks if you can and keep up your work productivity without over-exerting yourself by doing extra. You will have plenty of time to do extra once you are feeling back in the swing of things. And regardless of job position, try to get 7-8 hours of sleep each night.

Overeating may be another side effect of IF that you find yourself doing more often in the beginning stages, but this should decrease in frequency if you stay diligent about following a healthy eating plan [72] [73]. It may feel natural to assume that anything you eat after fasting is simply "making up for" the calories you did not consume while fasting. This is not true, and it negates the point of fasting to begin with. You are fasting to lose those hours of consumption (losing is a good thing in this scenario) because there are health and weight loss benefits tied to losing these hours of consumption. By overeating to "make up for" the calories not consumed during fasting, you risk diminishing or erasing these health and weight loss benefits altogether.

Without trying to induce heavy blushing, you may find yourself running to the restroom much more often than you are used to while practicing IF [73]. This is because you are drinking water all day long without consuming food for hours at a time, meaning the only substance in your stomach will be water. When you were eating normally throughout the day, you had food being digested to absorb most of the water which meant you probably used the restroom a few times throughout the day. Now, you may find yourself running to the restroom a few times an hour! While slightly inconvenient, this is normal, and you should not decrease your water intake while practicing IF just to reduce the number of bathroom trips you are taking. The best advice would be to make sure you have easy access to a bathroom and do not wait too long to relieve yourself. If you work at a job where you cannot leave your workstation frequently throughout the day, perhaps speak with a supervisor if it is not too embarrassing to let them know what is going on.

Feeling coldness in your fingers and toes is a common side effect of IF because fasting increases blood flow to fat stores tucked around the body [73]. The name for this is adipose blood tissue flow, and the purpose is to transfer fat into your muscles, where the fat will be burned as fuel or used as energy. Aside from adipose tissue flow, coldness is also a side effect of blood sugar dropping as a result of fasting. If you chill easily, you may want to layer your clothes and/or carry a jacket with you to the office, restaurant, movie theater, or other common destinations in your daily routine. You might also consider sipping hot coffee or tea as a zero-calorie beverage throughout the day. I personally swear by the space heater I have in my office; they are normally listed for a reasonable price at any large retail store.

Being "hangry" is a popular expression for a reason: feeling hungry may make you feel downright irritable [73]. This could be because of a culmination of other side effects like headaches, fatigue, cravings, and/or the effects of blood sugar levels dropping after extended periods without eating. Whatever the reason may be, you probably won't care when hanger strikes. Do yourself (and everyone around you) a favor and plan ahead for these moments. Pack a fun zero-calorie drink to enjoy or brew a cup of coffee for a pick-me-up. Remember that this feeling is temporary; yes, you will indeed eat again at some point. And in the meantime, avoid unpleasant interactions with co-workers, friends, and family who you know will only worsen the mood.

Cravings for unhealthy foods should die down as you settle into your IF routine and eat a balanced diet most of the time while indulging sporadically [72]. However, if I told you to avoid thinking about a chocolate chip cookie, chances are you are going to think about a chocolate chip cookie. We tend to want things we know are forbidden – even if they are not normally a part of our routine anyway! This may turn out to be true for you with fasting. If you know you are not supposed to eat, you may, in turn, be obsessed with the thought of eating and develop strong cravings for particular foods along the way. This is one reason why it is so important not to deprive yourself of indulgences once in a while. Chances are after you have gone so long without the indulgence and become accustomed to eating healthy, once you indulge the craving will be satisfied for some time.

Because your stomach normally produces acid to digest food, and you are digesting less food, especially during fasting, you may experience gastrointestinal symptoms like constipation, heartburn, and bloating [73]. Some of you may not experience any of these symptoms at all; however, some of you may experience one or more of these symptoms between mild to severe in the level of discomforts. To avoid or subdue the symptoms, make sure you are drinking plenty of water throughout the day especially during fasting periods. During nonfasting periods, it is imperative that you avoid greasy or otherwise heartburn-inducing foods like burgers, fries, pizza, and the like. For both fasting and nonfasting periods, one suggestion is to prop yourself up while sleeping perhaps by using two or three pillows to keep your head above your waist during shut-eye [73].

Factors To Success

You made it! This is the final chapter of this book. So far, you have been successful in taking what is likely your first step toward implementing IF into your new, healthy lifestyle change. Now it is up to you to go out into the world and actually use all the knowledge you have acquired about IF and take action. This may seem daunting, especially for those of you who have not been in the swing of healthy eating and/or exercise in a long time. Don't worry; take it slow. If you know anything by now it is that you should ease into IF and not only pick a type of IF that fits your lifestyle, but adjust the type of IF you choose throughout time to ensure it keeps fitting your lifestyle as things inevitably change. In this chapter, I'm going to give you some realistic, simple factors that you can practice to help improve the chance that your IF journey is a success.

Have The Right Mindset

If anything is learned from this book, may it be that IF is a lifestyle change [55]. This is not a diet to jump into full-force only to give up a week in because too much was taken on too soon. Take time to figure out which IF type works best for you and ease into it by starting with shorter fasts before working toward longer fasts. Keep the mindset that IF is an iterative practice rather than set in stone, i.e., if one method of IF does not work for you, adjust the plan and keep trying until you find a method that works best for your individual needs.

Practicing IF should not be a painful experience, but rather a healthy lifestyle change that you are making for yourself to look and feel your best. Be mindful that someone else's best may not be the same as your best. Try not to compare your personal progress with others you know who practice IF, or with health and fitness bloggers online. These people may be following a different type of IF than you, consuming different foods than you, exercising differently than you, and so forth. What matters the most is that your preferred type of IF gets you the results you need.

Plan Ahead

Planning ahead is crucial for any diet plan, but for IF in particular, it is important to plan ahead to avoid some of the common pitfalls we just discussed earlier. Having healthy snacks on-hand, nutritious meals prepared ahead of time, and a water bottle within arm's length at all times is key to staying on track in your IF journey. While it would be impossible to anticipate every possible scenario, challenge yourself to think of the most ironic, funniest, or least entertaining places a hunger pang might strike. For example, it would be awful for this to happen in the middle of bumper-to-bumper traffic with no exit in sight. Having the foresight to plant snacks in your car, your purse, or pockets to avoid this situation would be golden.

Life is hectic, and sometimes events come up at the last minute. Having a snack on-hand will not only prevent you from overeating at an impromptu lunch meeting or dinner out with friends, but it will also be a lifesaver on days you might feel overly hungry during a fast and water is not helping. Nutritious meals prepared ahead of time are similarly lifesaving because, although your body will adjust to fasting over time, it will deter you from reaching for the first quick bite you find that may not always be nutrient-friendly. And speaking of friendly, water will become your best friend during IF. This is because sometimes when you feel hungry, you are actually thirsty. It is a good idea to take a nice gulp of water and wait several minutes to discern whether the feeling of hunger is still present or whether water was what your body was craving.

Realistic Expectations

While weight loss is likely after practicing IF for some time, the practice of IF is not magic [56]. Unfortunately, pounds are not going to fall off at a rapid pace such that drastic results will be seen immediately. In fact, if this is the case, there is something wrong, and you should seek immediate medical attention. Along with having the right mindset, having appropriate expectations of what IF is going to take from and bring to your life is imperative to your success.

Before you begin IF, separate a sheet of blank paper into two halves by drawing a line down the middle of it. On the left-hand side of the paper, list the ideal goals you hope to achieve by practicing IF. On the right-hand side of the paper, list the *realistic* goals you foresee achieving by practicing IF. Now, compare the two lists and find the similarities as well as the differences. Do you think your ideal and realistic goals could meet in the middle? If so, try to find some common ground between the two so that you don't become completely disenfranchised while at the same time you are able to maintain a grounded approach to this new lifestyle.

Setbacks And How To Deal With Them

You have the right mindset, you have the snacks and meals prepared, and your expectations are on point, but your family unexpectedly came into town on a morning you are fasting and want to go to breakfast. Before smoke and sirens go off in your head, take a deep breath. You are going to experience a plethora of setbacks during this lifestyle change because your life is likely filled with obligations outside of your fasting schedule. This is perfectly normal! How you respond to these inevitable setbacks is what matters.

So, the family is in town, and you go to breakfast to spend time with them even though you should be fasting for another few hours. When things like this come up, realize that breaking one fast too early is not going to derail your entire lifestyle change. Eat your breakfast and start the next fast at the normal time you would have, had you not experienced the setback. In other words, if the schedule is broken, try to get back on the schedule as soon as you can.

There will also be cases when fasting at all is simply impossible, dangerous, or unreasonable. This could be for medical reasons, emergencies, training for a marathon, or other extreme circumstances. Depending on how long you will need to forego fasting, you may be able to jump right back into the routine as quickly as possible if it is a short-term delay. If a long-term delay, ease back into the routine with a modified version of the IF type and shorter fasting periods.

Staying Motivated

Whether you are 6 months deep into practicing IF and getting bored or 3 days in and getting bored, staying motivated to keep chugging along is imperative to your success in IF. Much of the sustainment of your motivation is going to depend on some of the factors to success we just talked about, in particular, the factor of having the right mindset. Look, losing weight and gaining health benefits from IF is not an overnight ordeal. You may lose motivation if you feel defeated by not seeing results after a week of IF. Recall that IF is a lifestyle change; this is the mindset we should have, right? In keeping this mindset of lifelong gains, you may not feel defeated because you understand that it may be several weeks before you visibly see results.

Staying motivated also has a lot to do with keeping realistic expectations. This goes hand-in-hand with having the right mindset because your expectations are dependent on the mindset you have. If your expectations are too drastic, you may not stay motivated if you do not reach these unrealistic expectations in your self-defined amount of time. However, if you adopt the mindset that your goals are long-term and adjust your expectations to achieve small, short-term goals that incrementally build up to your long-term goal, you may stay motivated to see the results. This is where mindfulness techniques, meditation, and exercise can come in handy because unrealistic expectations are often rooted in anxiety.

Speaking of mindfulness and meditation, be patient with yourself and your body as you embark on this new lifestyle. Stay motivated by staying in the moment. Focus on what you can do today to make the best out of your IF experience, whether it be going for a walk and enjoying the outdoors or trying a new food or meal if it is a nonfasting day. One of my favorite phrases is that the same amount of time will pass whether you are happy or miserable, so you may as well make the most out of the time you have. In addition to the good days where everything seems to be going right, and you enjoy your walks and new foods, try not to get disappointed on the bad days when you may need to break the fast too early or otherwise deviate from your fasting schedule because something comes up. If this happens, stay motivated by getting right back into your IF diet or fasting schedule at the next chance.

While it would be unhealthy to fixate so obsessively over your weight loss or health goals that it consumes your life, creating a vision board would be a great way to stay motivated. A vision board is a completely individualized creation that you could make either on a literal piece of cardboard, whiteboard, or sheet of paper by pasting images of what your goal is onto this surface. If your goal is to lose weight, your vision board might include pictures of healthy foods, swimsuits, an outfit you aspire to wear, an event you aspire to go to after you've lost weight (think: wedding), or anything else that you associate with your goal of weight loss. The purpose of a vision board is to plant this vision into your mind so tangibly that you manifest the vision into reality. This does not mean to create the vision board, then put it away and forget about it; rather, keep the vision board in an area of your home or office that you see every day and would inspire you to think deeply about the goal you have in mind.

If a vision board seems like too much work or you are not the creative type, you could still stay motivated by planting little tokens of motivation throughout the destinations of your day. For instance, you could print motivational quotes or pictures to keep on your refrigerator, so one of the first things you see in the morning reminds you to stay motivated in reaching your goal. You could also plant motivational messages on your bathroom mirror, in your shower, on the dashboard of your car, on your desk at work, or anywhere else you can think of. This may sound cheesy or even a bit juvenile, and I agree, some motivational pictures and quotes can be over-the-top cheese. However, the point is for you to personalize these motivational tidbits throughout your day such that they are tailored to whatever will keep you on track. Some people decide to lose weight because they are at risk of dying prematurely and do not want to leave their families behind so young; in this case, you might have pictures of your children spread throughout your day to remind you what you are practicing IF for.

Closing Remarks

These factors for success and tips on staying motivated genuinely helped me survive and thrive in my IF journey; I hope they will help you achieve your goals, too. At the same time, keep in mind that these suggestions are not a magic wand and some suggestions may work better for you than others. As you progress through your individual IF journey, you may discover your own secrets to success and methods for staying motivated that work just as well if not better than the ones that I've suggested. And, this is indicative of IF as a whole being completely tailored to you depending on your lifestyle and your needs. Hopefully, when you become the IF pro, you will be able to share your own survival tips to beginners in the same shoes you are now.

Conclusion

With the simplicity of structuring IF around any schedule, without calorie-counting or rigorous exercise required, it is no wonder why this lifestyle trend has exploded in popularity in recent decades. Unlike some other diet fads, IF has real health and weight loss benefits proven by research including disease prevention and insulin regulation that may have to do with the ability of IF to induce regenerative cellular processes. IF also promotes weight loss through calorie reduction and generally improving lifestyle habits which can lead to prevention of a whole host of obesity-related diseases. You don't have to starve, and you don't have to waste any more energy stressing about what to eat; IF is a long-term lifestyle commitment that you can design to fit into the life you already have.

Women respond differently to IF than men because the hormonal, caloric, and metabolic needs between the two sexes are not the same. This hardly means women cannot practice IF and hopefully by now there is no question about this fact. Women may simply need to modify their IF regimen to incorporate shorter and less frequent fasts than men, which is simple and easy to do with the 10-day starter sample provided in this book. Take the suggested foods, workouts, and mindfulness exercises and adapt them to your heart's desire to make sure you are maximizing the benefits of your personalized IF journey.

If ever you feel an aspect of your IF schedule or diet plan is not working for you, remember this is an iterative rather than a linear process. This means you may need to revisit and change things along the way like the times you are fasting, how long you are fasting, the foods you are eating, and the workouts that best fit with the fasting and dieting you have going on. This is a major life change, and as long as you approach it as a long-term learning process, using the tools in this book and all of the information available to you at your fingertips in this information-savvy day-in-age, I have no doubt that you will succeed.

References

1. Kerndt, P. R., Naughton, J. L., Driscoll, C. E., & Loxterkamp, D. A. (1982). Fasting: the history, pathophysiology and complications. *The Western Journal of Medicine, 137*(5), 379-99.

2. Persynaki, A., Karras, S., & Pichard, C. (2017). Unraveling the metabolic benefits of fasting related to religious beliefs: A narrative review. *Nutrition, 35,* 14-21.

3. Di Francesco, A., Di Germanio, C., Bernier, M., & de Cabo, R. (2018). A time to fast. *Science, 362,* 770-775.

4. Coyle, D. (2018, July 22). Intermittent fasting for women: A beginner's guide. Retrieved from https://www.healthline.com/nutrition/intermittent-fasting-for-women

5. Shah, A. (2016, May 22). The secret to intermittent fasting for women. Retrieved from https://draxe.com/intermittent-fasting-women/

6. Heilbronn, L.K., Civitarese, A.E., Bogacka, I., Smith, S.R., Hulver, M., & Ravussin, E. (2005). Glucose tolerance and skeletal muscle gene expression in response to alternate day fasting. *Obesity Research, 13*(3), 574-581.

7. Klempel, M.C., Kroeger, C.M., Bhutani, S., Trepanowski, J.F., & Varady, K. A. (2012). Intermittent fasting combined with calorie restriction is effective for weight loss and cardio-protection in obese women. *Nutrition Journal, 11,* 98. doi: 10.1186/1475-2891-11-98

8. Martin, B., Pearson, M., Kebejian, L., Keselman, A., Bender, M., Carlson, O., ...& Mattson, M.P. (2007). Sex-dependent metabolic, neuroendocrine, and cognitive responses to dietary energy restriction and excess. *Endocrinology, 148*(9), 4318-4333.

9. Martin, B., Pearson, M., Brenneman, R., Golden, E., Wood, W., Prabhu, V., ...& Maudsley, S. (2009). Gonadal transcriptome alterations in response to dietary energy intake: sensing the reproductive environment. *PloS One, 4*(1), e4146.

10. Meczekalski, B., Katulski, K., Podfigurna-Stopa, A. & Maciejewska-Jeske, M. (2014). Functional hypothalamic amenorrhea and its influence on women's health. *Journal of Endocrinological Investigation, 37*(11), 1049-1056. doi: 10.1007/s40618-014-0169-3

11. Korek, E., Krauss, H., Gibas-Dorna, M., Kupsz, J., Piątek, M., & Piątek, J. (2013). Fasting and postprandial levels of ghrelin, leptin and insulin in lean, obese and anorexic subjects. *Przeglad gastroenterologiczny, 8*(6), 383-9.

12. Kettle & Fire. (2018). Intermittent fasting for women: Your complete guide. Retrieved from

https://blog.kettleandfire.com/intermittent-fasting-for-women/

13. Kumar, S. & Kaur, G. (2013). Intermittent fasting dietary restriction regimen negatively influences reproduction in young rats: a study of hypothalamo-hypophysial-gonadal axis. *PloS One, 8*(1), e52416. doi: 10.1371/journal.pone.0052416

14. Rosenbaum, M., & Leibel, R. L. (2010). Adaptive thermogenesis in humans. *International Journal of Obesity, 34,* S47-55.

15. Patterson, R. E., Laughlin, G. A., LaCroix, A. Z., Hartman, S. J., Natarajan, L., Senger, C. M., Martínez, M. E., Villaseñor, A., Sears, D. D., Marinac, C. R., ... Gallo, L. C. (2015). Intermittent Fasting and Human Metabolic Health. *Journal of the Academy of Nutrition and Dietetics, 115*(8), 1203-12.

16. Zauner, C., Schneeweiss, B., Kranz, A., Madl, C., Ratheiser, K., Kramer, L., ...& Lenz, K. (2000).

Resting energy expenditure in short-term starvation is increased as a result of an increase in serum norepinephrine. *The American Journal of Clinical Nutrition, 71*(6), 1511-1515.

17. Kollias, H. (2018). Intermittent fasting for women: important information you need to know. Retrieved from https://www.precisionnutrition.com/intermittent-fasting-women

18. Nadolsky, S. (2018). Fitness & menstrual health: how to stay lean, healthy, and fit without losing your period. Retrieved from https://www.precisionnutrition.com/fitness-menstrual-health

19. Mauvais-Jarvis, F., Clegg, D. J., & Hevener, A. L. (2013). The role of estrogens in control of energy balance and glucose homeostasis. *Endocrine Reviews, 34*(3), 309-38.

20. Metabolic disturbance (n.d.) *WordNet 3.0, Farlex clipart collection*. (2003-2008). Retrieved from https://www.thefreedictionary.com/Metabolic+distu rbance

21. Collier, R. (2013). Intermittent fasting: the science of going without. *Canadian Medical Association Journal,185*(9), E363-4. doi: 10.1503/cmaj.109-4451

22. Longo, V. D., & Mattson, M. P. (2014). Fasting: molecular mechanisms and clinical applications. *Cell Metabolism, 19*(2), 181-92.

23. Glick, D., Barth, S., & Macleod, K. F. (2010). Autophagy: cellular and molecular mechanisms. *The Journal of Pathology, 221*(1), 3-12.

24. Rabinowitz, J. & White, E. (2010). Autophagy and metabolism. *Science, 330*, 1344-1348. doi: 10.1126/science.1193497

25. He, C., Sumpter, R., & Levine, B. (2012). Exercise induces autophagy in peripheral tissues and in the brain. *Autophagy, 8*(10), 1548-1551. doi: 10.4161/auto.21327

26. Li, L., Chen, Y., & Gibson, B. (2013). Starvation-induced autophagy is regulated by mitochondrial reactive oxygen species leading to AMPK activation. *Cellular Signalling, 25*(1), 50-65. https://doi.org/10.1016/j.cellsig.2012.09.020

27. Jing, K., & Lim, K. (2012). Why is autophagy important in human diseases?. *Experimental & Molecular Medicine, 44*(2), 69-72.

28. Mah, L.Y., & Ryan, K.M. (2012). Autophagy and cancer. *Cold Spring Harbor Perspectives in Biology, 4*(1), a008821. doi: 10.1101/cshperspect.a008821.

29. Wheless, J.W. (2008). History of the ketogenic diet. *Epilepsia, 49* (s8), 3-5. https://doi.org/10.1111/j.1528-1167.2008.01821.x

30. Foster, D.W. & McGarry, J.D. (1982). The regulation of ketogenesis. *Ciba Foundation Symposium, 87,* 120-131.

31. Martin, B., Mattson, M. P., & Maudsley, S. (2006). Caloric restriction and intermittent fasting: two potential diets for successful brain aging. *Ageing Research Reviews, 5*(3), 332-53.

32. Zhou, W., Mukherjee, P., Kiebish, M. A., Markis, W. T., Mantis, J. G., & Seyfried, T. N. (2007). The calorically restricted ketogenic diet, an effective alternative therapy for malignant brain cancer. *Nutrition & Metabolism, 4,* 5. doi:10.1186/1743-7075-4-5

33. Fontán-Lozano, A., Saez-Cassanelli, J.L., Inda, M.C., de los Santos-Arteaga, M., Sierra-Dominguez, S.A., Lopez-Lluch, G., ...& Carrion, A.M. (2007). Caloric restriction increases learning consolidation and facilitates synaptic plasticity through mechanisms

dependent on NR2B subunits of the NMDA receptor. *Journal of Neuroscience, 27,*10185–10195.

34. Harvie, M. N., Pegington, M., Mattson, M. P., Frystyk, J., Dillon, B., Evans, G., ...& Howell, A. (2010). The effects of intermittent or continuous energy restriction on weight loss and metabolic disease risk markers: a randomized trial in young overweight women. *International Journal of Obesity, 35*(5), 714-27.

35. Mattson, M.P., Allison, D.B., Fontana, L., Harvie, M., Longo, V.D., Malaisse, W.J., ...& Panda, S. (2014). Meal frequency and timing in health and disease. *Proceedings of the National Academy of Sciences, 111*(47), 16647-16653.

36. Li, L., Wang, Z., & Zuo, Z. (2013). Chronic intermittent fasting improves cognitive functions and brain structures in mice. *PloS one, 8*(6), e66069. doi:10.1371/journal.pone.0066069

37. Lee, J., Seroogy, K.B., & Mattson, M.P. (2002). Dietary restriction enhances neurotrophin expression and neurogenesis in the hippocampus of adult mice. *Journal of Neurochemistry, 80*(3), 539-547.

38. Wang, B.H., Hou, Q., Lu, Y.Q., Jia, M.M., Qiu, T., Wang, X.H., ...& Jiang, Y. (2018). Ketogenic diet attenuates neuronal injury via autophagy and mitochondrial pathways in pentylenetetrazol-kindled seizures. *Brain Research, 1678,* 106-115.

39. De Bock, K., Derave, W., Eijnde, O., Hesselink, M.K., Koninckx, E., Rose, A.J., ...& Hespel, P. (2008). Effect of training in the fasted state on metabolic responses during exercise with carbohydrate intake. *Journal of Applied Physiology, 104,* 1045-1055. doi: 10.1152/japplphysiol.01195.2007

40. Hession, M., Rolland, C., Kulkarni, U., Wise, A., & Broom, J. (2009). Systematic review of randomized controlled trials of low-carbohydrate vs. low-fat/low-calorie diets in the management of obesity and its

comorbidities. *Obesity Reviews, 10*(1), 36-50. doi: 10.1111/j.1467-789X.2008.00518

41. Jabre, M.G., & Beijani, B.P. (2006). Treatment of Parkinson disease with diet-induced hyperketonemia: a feasibility study. *Neurology, 66*(4), 617. doi: 10.1212/01.wnl.0000216108.57529.b1

42. BBC News. (2018, February 19). A third of UK adults underestimate calorie intake. Retrieved from https://www.bbc.com/news/health-4311

43. Choi, B. C., Morrison, H., Wong, T., Wu, J., & Yan, Y. P. (2007). Bringing chronic disease epidemiology and infectious disease epidemiology back together. *Journal of Epidemiology and Community Health, 61*(9), 832.

44. Heilbronn L.K., & Ravussin E. (2003). Calorie restriction and aging: review of the literature and implications for studies in humans. *American Journal of Clinical Nutrition, 78,*361, 9.2790

45. Goodrick, C.L., Ingram, D.K., Reynolds, M.A., Freeman, J.R., & Cider, N. (1990). Effects of intermittent feeding upon body weight and lifespan in inbred mice: interaction of genotype and age. Mech Aging Dev, *55*, 69–87.

46. Willett, W.C., Koplan, J.P, Nugent, R., Dusenbury, C., Puska, P., & Gaziano, T.A. (2006). Prevention of chronic disease by means of diet and lifestyle changes. In: Jamison DT, Breman JG, Measham AR, et al., editors. *Disease Control Priorities in Developing Countries.* 2nd edition. Washington (DC): The International Bank for Reconstruction and Development / The World Bank. Chapter 44. Available from: https://www.ncbi.nlm.nih.gov/books/NBK11795/ Co-published by Oxford University Press, New York.

47. Centers for Disease Control and Prevention. (2017, November 28). Heart disease facts. Retrieved from https://www.cdc.gov/heartdisease/facts.htm

48. Stenkamp-Strahm, C. M., Nyavor, Y. E., Kappmeyer, A. J., Horton, S., Gericke, M., & Balemba, O. B. (2015). Prolonged high fat diet ingestion, obesity, and type 2 diabetes symptoms correlate with phenotypic plasticity in myenteric neurons and nerve damage in the mouse duodenum. *Cell and tissue research, 361*(2), 411-26.

49. Heilbronn, L.K., Smith, S.R., Martin, C.K., Anton, S.D., & Ravussin, E. (2005). Alternate-day fasting in nonobese subjects: effects on body weight, body composition, and energy metabolism. *American Journal of Clinical Nutrition, 81*(1), 69-73.

50. Barnosky, A.R., Hoddy, K.K., Unterman, T.G., & Varady, K.A. (2014). Intermittent fasting vs daily calorie restriction for type 2 diabetes prevention: a review of human findings. *Translational Research, 164*(4), 302-311. doi: 10.1016/j.trsl.2014.05.013

51. Hoddy, K. K., Kroeger, C. M., Trepanowski, J. F., Barnosky, A. R., Bhutani, S., & Varady, K. A. (2015). Safety of alternate day fasting and effect on disordered eating behaviors. *Nutrition journal, 14*, 44. doi:10.1186/s12937-015-0029-9

52. Wilson, R. A., Deasy, W., Stathis, C. G., Hayes, A., & Cooke, M. B. (2018). Intermittent Fasting with or without Exercise Prevents Weight Gain and Improves Lipids in Diet-Induced Obese Mice. *Nutrients, 10*(3), 346. doi:10.3390/nu10030346

53. Office of Disease Prevention and Health Promotion (2018, December 19). Current guidelines. Retrieved from https://health.gov/paguidelines/second-edition/

54. Siim Land. (2017, November 21). 3 of my best intermittent fasting hacks (not coffee). Retrieved from siimland.com/my-best-intermittent-fasting-hacks/

55. Silas, & Grace. (n.d.). 8 intermittent fasting hacks that'll making your life easier. Retrieved from https://www.chasingfoxes.com/8-intermittent-fasting-hacks-thatll-making-your-life-easier/

56. Ninjaman. (2011, September 30). Top 17 sneaky intermittent fasting tricks. Retrieved from www.thefatlossninja.com/top-17-intermittent-fasting-tricks/

57. FastDay. (2014, April 4). When and what should I eat during intermittent fasting? Retrieved from https://www.fastday.com/fasting/getting-started-fasting/when-and-what-should-i-eat-when-intermittent-fasting/

58. Bubbs, M. (n.d.). 7 scientifically-backed benefits of intermittent fasting. Retrieved from https://blog.paleohacks.com/intermittent-fasting-benefits/

59. Gunnars, K. (2018, March 15). 6 health benefits of apple cider vinegar, backed by science. Retrieved from https://www.healthline.com/nutrition/6-proven-health-benefits-of-apple-cider-vinegar

60. Swithers, S.E. & Davidson, T.L. (2008). A role for sweet taste: calorie predictive relations in energy regulation by rats. *Behavioral Neuroscience,122*(1):161–173.

61. Anton, S. D., Martin, C. K., Han, H., Coulon, S., Cefalu, W. T., Geiselman, P., & Williamson, D. A. (2010). Effects of stevia, aspartame, and sucrose on food intake, satiety, and postprandial glucose and insulin levels. *Appetite, 55*(1), 37-43.

62. Zellman, K.M. (2010). Diet myth or truth: chewing gum for weight loss. Retrieved from https://www.webmd.com/diet/obesity/features/diet-myth-or-truth-chewing-gum-for-weight-loss#1

63. National Sleep Foundation. (n.d.). Scary ways technology affects your sleep. Retrieved from https://www.sleep.org/articles/ways-technology-affects-sleep/

64. European Society of Endocrinology. (2017, May 22). Sleep loss affects your waistline. *ScienceDaily*. Retrieved December 22, 2018 from www.sciencedaily.com/releases/2017/05/170522081 109.htm

65. Hardick, B.J. (2016, November 23). Simple hacks to optimize intermittent fasting. Retrieved from http://www.drhardick.com/intermittent-fasting-hacks

66. Lefave, S. (2018, June 25). 8 major mistakes people make when intermittent fasting. Retrieved from https://whatsgood.vitaminshoppe.com/intermittent-fasting-mistakes/

67. Toffelmire, A. (n.d.). Appetite vs. hunger. Retrieved from https://www.medbroadcast.com/channel/nutrition/diets-and-specific-foods/appetite-vs-hunger

68. Iron Disorders Institute. (2009). Iron-out-of balance in women. Retrieved from www.irondisorders.org/women

69. Cole, W.D. (n.d.). Intermittent fasting: a complete guide to benefits, diet plans & meals. Retrieved from https://www.mindbodygreen.com/articles/intermittent-fasting-diet-plan-how-to-schedule-meals

70. MacDonald, A. (2010, October 19). Why eating slowly may help you feel full faster. Retrieved from https://www.health.harvard.edu/blog/why-eating-slowly-may-help-you-feel-full-faster-20101019605

71. Sifferlin, A. (2012, February 2). How people-pleasing may lead to overeating. Retrieved from

healthland.time.com/2012/02/02/how-people-pleasing-leads-to-overeating/

72. Syuki, B. (2018, January 22). 12 side effects of intermittent fasting to keep in mind. Retrieved from https://www.curejoy.com/content/side-effects-of-intermittent-fasting/

73. Sugar, J. (2018, January 17). 9 common side effects of intermittent fasting (and how to deal). Retrieved from https://www.yahoo.com/lifestyle/9-common-side-effects-intermittent-013529487.html

Disclaimer

The information contained in this book and its components, is meant to serve as a comprehensive collection of strategies that the author of this book has done research about. Summaries, strategies, tips and tricks are only recommendations by the author, and reading this book will not guarantee that one's results will exactly mirror theauthor's results.

The author of this book has made all reasonable efforts to provide current and accurate information for the readers of this book. The author and its associates will not be held liable for any unintentional errors or omissions that may be found.

The material in the book may include information by third parties. Third party materials compriseof opinions expressed by their owners. As such, the author of this book does not assume responsibility or liability for any third party material or opinions.

The publication of third party material does not constitute the author's guarantee of any information, products, services, or opinions contained within third party material. Use of third party material does not guarantee that your results will mirror our results. Publication of such third party material is simply a recommendation and expression of the author's own opinion of that material.

Whether becauseof the progression of the Internet, or the unforeseen changes in company policy and editorial submission guidelines, what is stated as fact at the time of this writing may become outdated or inapplicable later.

written expressed and signed permission from the author.

Made in the USA
Middletown, DE
25 August 2020